Pebble® Plus

All About

Whale Sharks

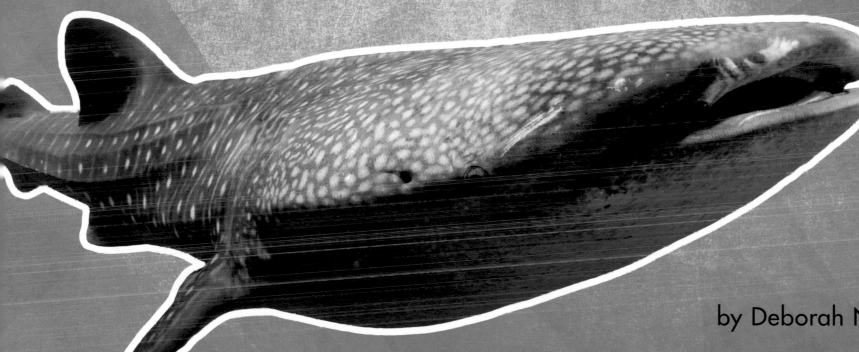

by Deborah Nuzzolo

raintree
a Capstone company — publishers for children

Raintree is an imprint of Capstone Global Library Limited, a company incorporated in England and Wales having its registered office at 264 Banbury Road, Oxford, OX2 7DY – Registered company number: 6695582

www.raintree.co.uk
myorders@raintree.co.uk

Edited by Nikki Clapper
Designed by Kayla Rossow
Picture research by Kelly Garvin
Production by Gene Bentdahl
Originated by Capstone Library Ltd
Printed and bound in China

ISBN 978 1 4747 4306 8
21 20 19 18 17
10 9 8 7 6 5 4 3 2 1

British Library Cataloguing in Publication Data
A full catalogue record for this book is available from the British Library.

Acknowledgements
We would like to thank the following for permission to reproduce photographs: Minden Pictures: Peter Verhoog/Buiten-beeld, 17, Reinhard Dirscheri, 13; Shutterstock: belizediversity, 1, divedog, 24, Dudarev Mikhail, 15, kaschibo, 9, kataleewan intarachote, 2, Krzysztof Odziomek, cover, 5, Rich Carey, 21, SeraphP, 19, Thanakon S, 7, Willyam Bradberry, 23; Superstock/FLPA, 11; Artistic elements: Shutterstock: Apostrophe, HorenkO, Magenta10

Every effort has been made to contact copyright holders of material reproduced in this book. Any omissions will be rectified in subsequent printings if notice is given to the publisher.

All the internet addresses (URLs) given in this book were valid at the time of going to press. However, due to the dynamic nature of the internet, some addresses may have changed, or sites may have changed or ceased to exist since publication. While the author and publisher regret any inconvenience this may cause readers, no responsibility for any such changes can be accepted by either the author or the publisher.

Contents

Giant of the sea

A huge shark swims
slowly in the sea.
It opens its wide mouth.
It pulls in tiny sea animals.
This is a whale shark.

Whale sharks are
the world's largest fish.
They live in warm seas.
These gentle giants are
not dangerous to people.

Lots of spots

Whale sharks have a long body and a wide, flat head. The mouth can be 1.5 metres (5 feet) wide.

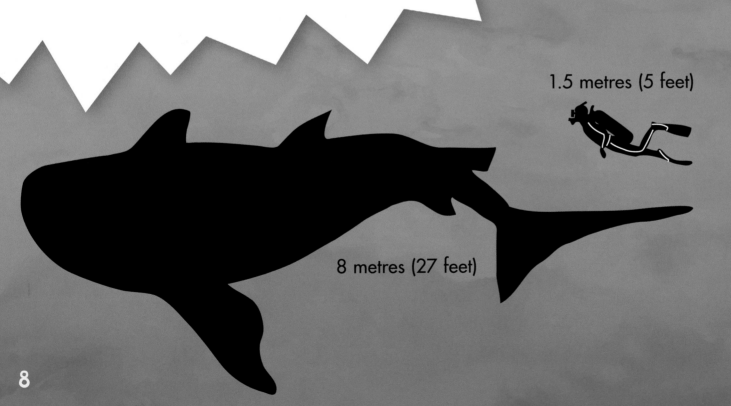

1.5 metres (5 feet)

8 metres (27 feet)

8

A whale shark is grey
with a white belly.
It has lots of spots.
Its eyes are small.

The skeleton of a
whale shark bends easily.

It is made of cartilage.

Cartilage is softer than bone.

Eating

Whale sharks are big,

but their food is small.

They eat tiny plants and

animals called plankton.

They also eat fish and squid.

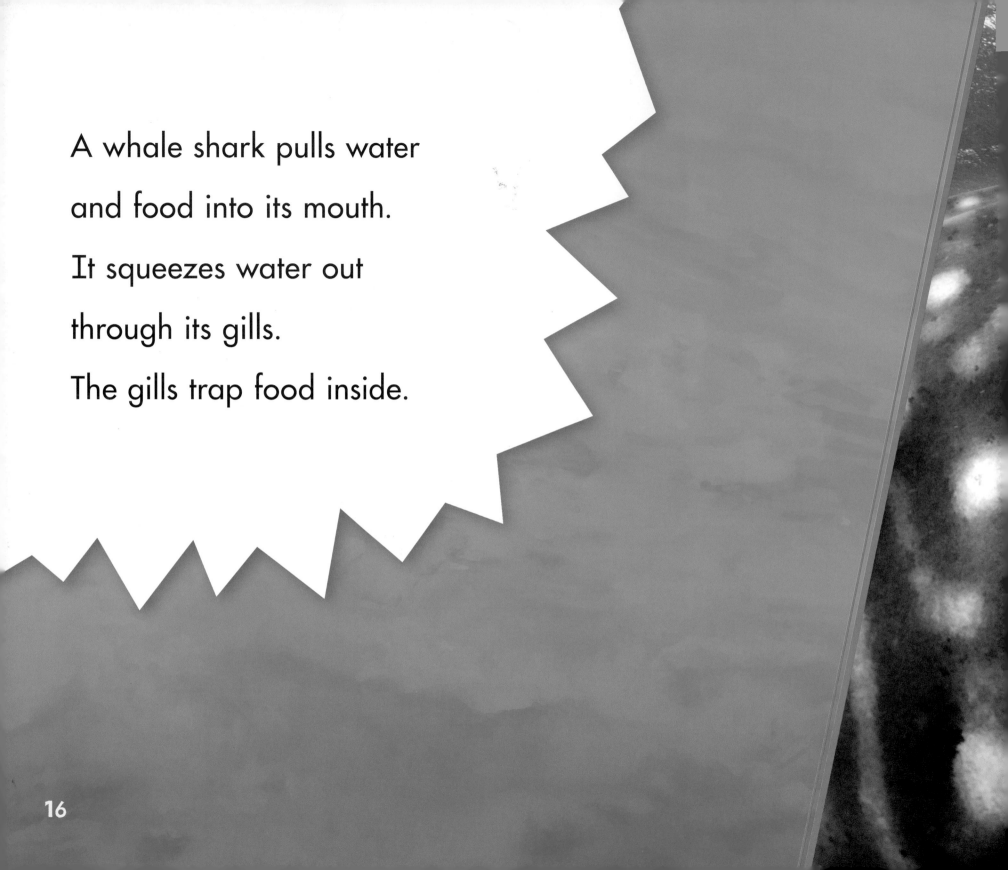

A whale shark pulls water
and food into its mouth.
It squeezes water out
through its gills.
The gills trap food inside.

gills

Whale shark babies

Whale shark pups hatch
from eggs inside their mother.
Up to 300 pups are born
at one time.

The pups are more than
61 centimetres (2 feet) long.
They live on their own.
Whale sharks live
for 70 years or longer.

Glossary

cartilage strong, bendable material that forms some body parts on humans and other animals

dangerous likely to cause harm or injury

gentle kind and calm

gill body part on the side of a fish; fish use their gills to breathe

hatch break out of an egg

plankton tiny plants and animals that drift in the sea

pup young shark

skeleton bones that support and protect the body of a human or other animal

squid sea animal with a long, soft body and 10 fingerlike arms used to grasp food

Find out more

Books

DK Findout! Sharks, DK (DK Publishing, 2017)

Encyclopedia of Dolphins, Sharks and Whales, North Parade (North Parade Publishing, 2014)

Whale Shark (Discover Sharks), Camilla Bédoyère (QED Publishing, 2013)

Websites

www.bbc.co.uk/programmes/p02n7s0d/clips
Watch lots of amazing videos of sharks in action at this BBC website.

www.worldwildlife.org/species/whale-shark
Learn why the whale shark is an endangered species at this World Wildlife Fund website.

Comprehension questions

1. How do whale sharks eat?

2. What is cartilage? How does cartilage help whale sharks move?

3. What do you think it would be like to swim with a whale shark?

Index